peculiar proverbs

Peculiar proverbs

weird words of wisdom from around the world

Stephen Arnott

St. Martin's Press · New York

www.stmartins.com

Illustrations by Kath Walker

Library of Congress Cataloging-in-Publication Data

Arnott, Stephen.
Peculiar proverbs : weird words of wisdom from around the world / Stephen Arnott.—1st U.S. ed.
p. cm.
ISBN-13: 978-0-312-38707-5
ISBN-10: 0-312-38707-5
1. Proverbs. I. Title.
PN6405.A76 2008
808.88—dc22
2008025774

First published in Great Britain by Summersdale Publishers Ltd

First U.S. Edition: December 2008

10 9 8 7 6 5 4 3 2 1

CONTENTS

INTRODUCTION

The proverbs in this book are all genuine sayings collected from many cultures around the world. They are extracts from a number of proverb collections (many dating from the nineteenth century) compiled by various folklorists, linguists, social anthropologists and travellers.

Many common proverbs, though wise, can be a little on the dull side ('Great minds think alike', 'Honesty is the best policy', 'Look before you leap' etc.). This collection ignores the common sayings we're all familiar with and concentrates on the more colourful, unusual and, in some cases, incomprehensible proverbs that have been recorded over the years.

Many of these sayings fall naturally into categories such as 'Love and Marriage' or 'The Fairer Sex' but others are not so easy to classify and have been ordered in a less conventional fashion. Many of my favourite sayings are gathered in the first chapter 'A Nice Turn of Phrase' (With patience and saliva the ant swallows an elephant); some proverbs are frankly baffling, to me at any rate (A mother-in-law near the door is like a cloak near a hedge), and many of these are included in 'Say Again?' Others appear distinctly odd at first glance, but with a bit of thought reveal a nugget of wisdom (What a pleasure to sit in the fire, having on strange trousers), these have been included in 'Hidden Depths?' Of course, what is baffling to me might be blindingly obvious to you, and vice versa, so please forgive any inconsistencies.

I hope you enjoy *Peculiar Proverbs* and remember... The man who tickles himself can laugh when he chooses.

Stephen Arnott

A NICE TURN OF PHRASE

A mixed bag of deft, colourful and evocative sayings on a variety of subjects.

Never bolt your door with a boiled carrot.
IRISH

The quiet duck puts his foot on
the unobservant worm.
CHINESE

Only a pumpkin is a head without cares.
ITALIAN

Better be the beak of a chicken
than the rump of an ox.
CHINESE

Poets and pigs are only appreciated
after their death.
ITALIAN

11

Words are mere bubbles of water,
but deeds are drops of gold.
TIBETAN

It is better to suffer the satiated mosquito
to stay than to admit the hungry one.
SERBIAN

One sprinkles the most sugar
where the tart is burnt.
DUTCH

You cannot prevent the birds of sadness
from flying over your head, but you can
prevent them from nesting in your hair.
CHINESE

He sits full still that has riven trousers.
SCOTTISH

Other people's goats always
have the biggest udders.
LATIN

It's a hard job to make old
monkeys pull new faces.
FLEMISH

Hope is the dream of waking.
DANISH

13

Do not stab yourself because
you have a golden knife.
MARATHI (INDIA)

The man who spends the night in a
marsh wakes a cousin to the frogs.
TUNISIAN

To carry a light when the moon
shines makes tigers laugh.
MALAYAN

After being struck on the head by an
axe, it is a positive pleasure to be beaten
about the body with a wooden club.
CHINESE

14

The shrimp that sleeps is carried
away by the current.
CHILEAN

It is easy to cut whangs off
other folks' leather.
SCOTTISH

Don't be after breaking your shin
on a stool that isn't there.
IRISH

The beetle in its hole is a sultan.
EGYPTIAN

15

A centipede doesn't stop for a game leg.
BURMESE

Mistakes ain't haystacks or there'd
be more fat ponies than there is.
NORTH AMERICAN

With patience and saliva the
ant swallows an elephant.
COLOMBIAN

It is nobler to be taken by a big crocodile
than to be nibbled to pieces by little fishes.
MALAYAN

Fowl scratch up too much dirt, him run
risk of finding him grandma's skeleton.
JAMAICAN

Many shrimps, many flavours;
many men, many whims.
MALAYAN

Alms once given are as phlegm which has
been expectorated – not worth taking back.
KUMAONI (INDIA)

A spur in the head is worth two in the heel.
SCOTTISH

Nothing to bother you, eh?
Then go and buy a goat.
INDIAN

Sycophants scratch pimples for a livelihood.
TELEGU (INDIA)

A lame cat is better than a swift
horse when rats infest the palace.
CHINESE

Dogs and rude people have no hands.
ITALIAN

A naked man can be seen from afar;
a rude one, close at hand.
LATVIAN

He who does evil to a benefactor is
like a dog which eats up the piece
of leather on which he sleeps.
INDIAN

Farming, letter writing, worship and the
tightening of your horse's girth; these
things should be done by yourself, though
you have a hundred thousand attendants.
PUNJABI

It is a sick duck that is worried by the weasel.
CHINESE

19

A man that pets a live catfish
ain't crowded with brains.
NORTH AMERICAN

Death is a black camel that
kneels at every man's gate.
TURKISH

The tongue is soft and constantly remains
in; the teeth are hard and fall out.
CHINESE

If you do what people tell you, you
will be fishing hares in the sea and
hunting fish in the woods.
BULGARIAN

The dragon in shallow water
becomes the butt of shrimps.
CHINESE

Mind your pullets, my cocks are abroad!
JERSEY

Our Lady of Pity and Mister Saint
Peter gave bad cows short horns.
BRETON

Although there exist many thousands
of subjects for elegant conversation,
there are persons who cannot meet a
cripple without talking about feet.
CHINESE

He that denies the cat skimmed milk
must give the mouse cream.
RUSSIAN

Who does not feed the dog, feeds the thief.
ESTONIAN

One should not peer into the mouth of a
presentation cow and look at its teeth.
BURMESE

Do not examine the reindeer given by the rich
man lest you find it to be without horns.
FINNISH

Better a sausage in the hand,
than a ham in the butchers.
POLISH

A slice of ham is better than
a fat pig in a dream.
GERMAN

A bird in the soup is better than
an eagle's nest in the desert.
CHINESE

ON THE TIP OF MY TONGUE

Some words on conversation, language and gossip, and the merits of keeping your trap shut!

If a chattering bird be not placed in the mouth,
vexation will not sit between the eyebrows.
CHINESE

He whose tongue is arrested by his
front teeth, will never offend.
UKRAINIAN

Tuck your shirt in-between your legs
and your tongue between your teeth.
POLISH

In the tongue there lurks a dragon's den
— no blood is seen yet it murders men.
CHINESE

25

Empty gossip jumps with one leg.
ESTONIAN

A gossip's mouth is the devil's mailbag.
WELSH

A joke ought to have sheep's
teeth, not a dog's.
CZECH

A kick is better than a tongue blow.
BRETON

Whilst the sheep bleats, it loses a mouthful.
FLEMISH

He who is first silent in a quarrel
belongs to a good family.
SLOVAKIAN

As long as the language lives,
the nation is not dead.
BOHEMIAN

Our language is one great salad.
ROMANIAN

He is truly a superior man who can look
upon a game of chess in silence.
CHINESE

The Devil himself was learning the
Basque language for seven years and
then he only learned three words.
BASQUE

WISDOM AND DISCRETION

All cultures seem to appreciate the value of intelligence – it's a pity there doesn't seem to be enough to go around.

Because there are fools, wise men look well.
JAPANESE

If one person tells thou hast asses'
ears, take no notice; should two tell
thee so, procure a saddle for thyself.
HEBREW

To him of good judgement, the sound of a
gnat suffices; but to him who lacks it, the
sound of an orchestra helps him not.
TURKISH

He who knows he is a fool is not a big fool.
CHINESE

31

It is better to sit with an owl
than to hop with a blackbird.
GERMAN

A fox knows much; a hedgehog one great thing.
GREEK

Do not jump high under a low ceiling.
CZECH

A wise man wavers, a fool is fixed.
SCOTTISH

One is received according to one's coat;
one is dismissed according to one's brain.
RUSSIAN

When you go to a donkey's house,
don't talk about ears.
JAMAICAN

The bull-frog knows more about
rain than the almanac.
NORTH AMERICAN

He who can read and write has four eyes.
ALBANIAN

Do not blow in a bear's ear.
CZECH

When an ass climbs a ladder, we
may find wisdom in women.
HEBREW

The wise get a sledge in summer
and a carriage in winter.
PORTUGUESE

Do not speak of secret matters in
a field that is full of little hills.
HEBREW

The walls have mice and the mice have ears.
IRAQI

It is better to grumble into the
beard than into the air.
GERMAN

Thy friend has a friend, and thy friend's
friend has a friend: be discreet.
HEBREW

When your head does not
work, your legs suffer.
ROMANIAN

In the sweat of the forehead there is profit;
in the sweat of the neck there is none.
TSWANA (SOUTH AFRICA)

It is easy to be wise for yesterday.
RUSSIAN

If a man knew where he would fall
he would spread straw first.
FINNISH

COURAGE AND CAUTION

It's hard to be a hero – the advice seems to be to play it safe (or invest in a pair of running shoes).

He who has no courage must have legs.
ITALIAN

Caution is no cowardice, even fleas are armed.
UKRAINIAN

He who licks the saucepans at
home will not be killed in battle.
CZECH

Caution is the mother of the porcelain chest.
GERMAN

He who has burnt his mouth with
milk, blows on ice-cream.
TURKISH

Sheltered by a wall even an old
woman becomes courageous.
CZECH

He who speaks ill of you in your absence
fears you in your presence.
SPANISH

Three things cross the road to avoid:
a falling tree, your chief and second
wife whispering in agreement, and a
goat wearing a leopard's tail.
CHINESE

He's awful big behind the door.
SCOTTISH

41

Even mice may bite dead cats.
GERMAN

A fly that bites the tortoise breaks its beak.
ITALIAN

The egg that stops with its
master does not get broken.
ETHIOPIAN

The lame duck should avoid the ploughed field.
CHINESE

42

WORK (AND REASONS NOT TO)

Is hard work all it's cracked up to be? Some suggest you put your feet up; others point out the pitfalls of the 'relaxed' approach.

One is more likely to get hunch-
backed than rich through work.
RUSSIAN

No food was ever cooked by
gay clothes and frivolity.
FIJIAN

If one became rich through hard work, a
donkey would have a packsaddle of gold.
FRENCH

A new servant works hard but twenty days.
JAPANESE

Dry pants catch no fish.
BULGARIAN

He who would sweep the hut
must not sit on the broom.
BANTU (SOUTH/CENTRAL AFRICA)

A woman without a baby has no
excuse for sitting down.
IRISH

Fair words butter no cabbage.
SERBIAN

Two soldiers, nine captains.
CROATIAN

God is a good worker, but he
loves to be helped.
BASQUE

He who sleeps the red from the sun,
sleeps the fat from the cabbage.
DANISH

The ground is always frozen for lazy pigs.
DANISH

He who does not wish to soil his hands
and feet will have inactive teeth.
ALBANIAN

Lazy people are always anxious
to be doing something.
FRENCH

Laziness goes so slowly that
poverty overtakes it.
DUTCH

If you're naked, it's cold everywhere; if
you're lazy, it's hard everywhere.
LATVIAN

The peasant's eyes do more than his hands.
SWEDISH

Before dinner let us explore the
Southern Plains and climb the Northern
Mountains; after dinner there are snakes
in the Southern Plains and there are
tigers in the Northern Mountains.
CHINESE

The grimness of labour is better
than the saffron of sloth.
EGYPTIAN

You may serve a hundred years, but
you will not earn a hundred turnips.
RUSSIAN

He wants roasted larks to fall
from the sky on his plate.
ALBANIAN

Roast doves fly into no-one's mouths.
GERMAN

FOOD, GLORIOUS FOOD

Some eat, drink and get merry – others develop a bad case of indigestion.

More people are drowned in the
glass than in the sea.
LATVIAN

Avoid the tavern or limpets are your food.
IRISH

From four things God preserve us: a
painted woman, a conceited valet, salt beef
without mustard and a little late dinner.
INDIAN

The table, a secret thief, sends
its master to the hospital.
ITALIAN

One's own entrails prove worms to oneself.
THAI

If you drink you die, if you don't drink
you die; so it is better to drink.
RUSSIAN

He's like a bagpipe – he never makes
a noise till his belly's full.
IRISH

There is no God like the throat, it
accepts offerings every day.
YORUBA (WEST AFRICA)

You cannot drink water, it is not vodka.
RUSSIAN

Cabbage cooked twice is death.
GREEK

Whoever is king, tea is queen.
IRISH

He who is not tipsy on Sunday is not
worth shaking hands with on Monday.
ALBANIAN

54

When they tell you you are drunk,
hold by the wall and go on.
GREEK

Eat leeks in March, garlic in May: all the
rest of the year the doctors may play.
ENGLISH

Two cannot dine off one mouse.
UKRAINIAN

In the steppe even a beetle is meat.
RUSSIAN

Herring is in the land, the doctor's at a stand.
DUTCH

He who eats apples every day takes
the doctor's bread away.
CZECH

An apple at night puts the dentist to flight.
ENGLISH

For the invalid, a doctor; for
the healthy, a sausage.
ESTONIAN

No herring, no wedding.
MANX

When you see a village with nine
houses and ten inns, flee from it.
BULGARIAN

The stomach teaches the Laplander to shoot.
FINNISH

Click the teeth and the stomach
will open the door.
GEORGIAN

He who does not eat cheese will go mad.
FRENCH

It is easier to drink two glasses
than excuse yourself from one.
POLISH

Rest after a meal, even if
your parents are dead.
JAPANESE

Lower the sword and raise the glass.
POLISH

One does an old man no wrong
when one steals his supper.
GERMAN

When the food tastes best, stop eating.
SLOVAKIAN

THE TRUTH – AND NOTHING BUT...

According to many of the following, honesty is not always the best policy.

Tell the truth and try to escape.
UKRAINIAN

He who speaks the truth should
have one foot in the stirrup.
HINDI

At the near end of the market, he told a
lie; at the far end, he himself believed it.
TURKISH

Renounce the Devil, and thou
shalt wear a shabby cloak.
SPANISH

In the pool of lies only dead fish swim.
RUSSIAN

Folks like the truth that hits their neighbours.
NORTH AMERICAN

He who fiddles with the truth gets
the bow thrown at his head.
GERMAN

A thieving cow doesn't miss a gap.
COLOMBIAN

What everybody says must be true.
IRISH

To tell the truth is dangerous;
to listen to it is annoying.
DANISH

What smoke is to the eyes, and vinegar
is to the teeth, is truth to the ears.
GERMAN

Better a lie that heals than
a truth that wounds.
BOHEMIAN

You cannot handle honey without
licking your fingers.
SLOVENIAN

Lying a little and stealing a little will
get you nicely through the world.
ESTONIAN

There is no stranger who isn't well born,
nor old man who wasn't brave.
SPANISH

God, what things a man sees when
he goes out without a gun!
AFRIKAANS

Tell your friend a lie, and if he keeps
it a secret, tell him the truth.
ENGLISH

An egg-stealer will at last develop
into a camel-stealer.
IRAQI

One who is tempted today by a cucumber
will be tempted tomorrow by a goat.
KUMAONI (INDIA)

A lie well told is worth more
than a stupid fact.
ITALIAN

66

Of ten bald men, nine are deceitful
and the tenth is dumb.
CHINESE

Every man honest till the day they catch him.
JAMAICAN

A well-tinted lie counts as the truth.
SWEDISH

The custom of anglers: if a fish
escape – it was a big one!
MALAYAN

One who steals a little is hanged; one
who steals much goes by carriage.
ESTONIAN

SUCCESS AND
SOCIAL CLIMBERS

*Most people aim to get ahead in life, but
the social ladder can be very slippery.*

He who climbs up is easily seized by the heels.
GERMAN

Buttered bread falls on its face.
HEBREW

The cat knows well whose beard it licks.
FRENCH

When a dainty lady lives well, she
takes a pin to eat a pea.
JAMAICAN

When a peasant becomes a nobleman he
looks at the plough through spectacles.
GERMAN

Even when seated on a golden chair,
the frog jumps back to its puddle.
DUTCH

The smaller the lizard, the greater
its hope of becoming a crocodile.
ETHIOPIAN

Be a head, though only the head of a potato.
JAPANESE

I proud, and thou proud; who
shall carry the dirt out?
SWEDISH

If I be a queen, and thou be a queen;
who will bang the butter?
PUNJABI

I am a gentleman, you are a gentleman;
who is going to mind the swine?
CZECH

If I am to be a prince, and you are to be
a prince; who is to drive the donkey?
EGYPTIAN

Father a grocer; son a gentleman;
grandson a beggar.
PERUVIAN

Don't be deceived by the whiteness of the
turban: soap can be bought on credit.
TURKISH

When one acquires fame one
soon ceases to merit it.
HEBREW

He who eats cherries with his superiors
will have the pips thrown in his face.
DANISH

There is no art in becoming a peasant;
the art is to remain one.
DUTCH

He who advances by leaps and bounds, by
leaps and bounds falls into the ditch.
MALAYALAM (INDIA)

When God wills the destruction
of an ant, he gives it wings.
IRAQI

If a lowbred man obtains wealth, he
will carry an umbrella at midnight.
TAMIL

Be the husband only as big as an ant, yet
the wife seats herself amongst the great.
HEBREW

When the lower palm leaf falls, let
not the upper palm leaves laugh.
MALAYAN

The world is like a Turkish bath, the higher one sits, the more one sweats.
GERMAN

HUMAN NATURE

A selection of sayings on the many facets of the human condition — mostly the unsavoury ones.

If a fool has a hump, nobody notices
it; if the wise man has a pimple,
everybody talks about it.
RUSSIAN

What you can't have, abuse.
ITALIAN

Kiss the hand you cannot bite.
ROMANIAN

He who fondles you more than usual has
either deceived you, or wishes to do so.
FRENCH

If two men keep a horse, it is thin; if
two families keep a boat, it leaks.
CHINESE

Everything forbidden is sweet.
EGYPTIAN

Caress the dog so that he may
soil you with his paws.
ALBANIAN

Everyone is affable until a cow
goes into his garden.
IRISH

When the mouth has eaten its stomach
full, then the flour is bitter.
LIVONIAN

Scabby donkeys scent each
other over nine hills.
BULGARIAN

Praise and cabbage have a nice
taste, but they inflate.
POLISH

The news has been heard all round, but
the party it most concerns is deaf.
YORUBA (WEST AFRICA)

When the deaf man gives the blind
man a lamp, he receives bagpipes.
GERMAN

If one hundred men call a sage
a fool, he becomes one.
ALBANIAN

First he asks for your walking stick,
then he wants your pet daughter.
KASHMIRI (INDIA)

To the merry man, every weed is a flower; to
the afflicted man, every flower is a weed.
FINNISH

A man's own smell is unknown to him.
KALMYK (RUSSIA)

One is not smelt where all stink.
LATIN

Two-thirds of fame is in the skull.
WELSH

One hears pedestrians sing
most of the riding songs.
RUSSIAN

All things anger you and the
cat breaks your heart.
SCOTTISH

If the mistress breaks it, it is an accident;
if the servant breaks it, it is a fault.
KURDISH

The marvellous and the astonishing
only surprise for a week.
ETHIOPIAN

If you don't like headaches, have
less to do with other people.
SERBIAN

If you throw cakes at a man, he
will throw cakes at you.
JAPANESE

Need will make the old woman trot.
GUERNSEY

To be a complete man one should have
spent three years at a public school,
one at a university and two in prison.
RUSSIAN

He who would drown his dog,
first calls him mad.
FRENCH

The small man thinks that small acts of
goodness are of no benefit — and does not
do them; and that small deeds of evil do no
harm — and does not abstain from them.
CHINESE

He who builds by the wayside
will have many critics.
CZECH

A hog who has wallowed in the mud
seeks a clean person to rub against.
YORUBA (WEST AFRICA)

When you have figs in your haversack
everybody seeks your friendship.
ALBANIAN

Friends stick to you in harvest,
but fall off in summer.
MAORI

Heaps of people recollect favours by
marking them down in the snow.
NORTH AMERICAN

The giant loves the dwarf.
ENGLISH

Whatever you do not understand, you admire.
CROATIAN

The string of a man's sack of patience
is generally tied with a slipknot.
JAPANESE

STATING THE OBVIOUS?

One expects a proverb to contain a revealing insight. However, in many cases what counts as a proverb appears to be only a bland statement of fact. Is this advice as obvious as it looks, or is there a deeper meaning?

89

The he-goat is hard to milk.
CZECH

You may ride a horse well, but
don't try to sit on its nose.
BAMBARA (WEST AFRICA)

Do not remove a fly from your friend's
forehead with a hatchet.
CHINESE

One must walk a long time behind a wild duck
before one picks up an ostrich feather.
DANISH

When the bed is small, lie in the centre.
SPANISH

God preserve us from pitchforks,
for they make three holes.
SWISS

A cow pat is wider when trodden on.
IRISH

Once cannot go to heaven with
tallow-greased skis.
FINNISH

Being a baker is poor work if your
head is made of butter.
DANISH

Better to bring a case before the judge's
beard, than to the elbow-bone.
IRISH

He whose head is beeswax must
not go out in the sun.
SLOVENIAN

A crab does not beget a bird.
GA (WEST AFRICA)

If the rubbish heap of the barber is
stirred, nothing but hair turns up.
TAMIL

He who has corns on his toes
is easily overtaken.
GERMAN

It is not common for hens to have pillows.
SCOTTISH

He who welcomes the camel
driver needs a big gate.
TURKISH

The sea is a bad inn.
GERMAN

It is easy to comb a little horse.
IRISH

Why should a man without a head want a hat?
CHILEAN

Rain which does not fall remains in the sky.
SICILIAN

The poor man and the fire do
not like to be poked.
OROMO (NORTH AFRICA)

It is no use throwing water at a drowned rat.
IRISH

One must let people talk
sense, since fish can't.
POLISH

The crumbs in thy neighbour's
beard are his own.
SCOTTISH

A short nose is soon picked.
GERMAN

So much dough — so many buns.
LATVIAN

The junk capsizes and the
shark has his belly full.
MALAYAN

He who doesn't eat garlic
hasn't a stinking mouth.
YIDDISH

Put your dates in the honey-pot – but don't
sink it afterwards in the mud of the Nile.
EGYPTIAN

Don't rub salt on a sore.
JAPANESE

Water does not help fried fish.
GERMAN

It is no use trying to sell a ring to a leper.
BAMBARA (WEST AFRICA)

Tangled hair wants a wide comb.
SERBIAN

He who spits towards the sky gets
it back into his own face.
THAI

A straight road has no turning.
EFÏK (WEST AFRICA)

Too far east is west.
DUTCH

Never feed a dog with corn, nor attempt to
pick your teeth with a pair of scissors.
CHINESE

Garlic may be pounded in an earthenware
saucepan, but it can be done only once.
CHINESE

He who has only his eyebrow for a
crossbow never can kill an animal.
YORUBA (WEST AFRICA)

If you have a nose you can wear a nose-ring.
MARATHI (INDIA)

In an empty room even an
epidemic finds nothing.
ESTONIAN

What is heaviest should weigh heaviest.
DUTCH

It is no use applying eye-medicine
from a two-storey window.
JAPANESE

Two arrows in the quiver are better than
one – and three are better still.
INDIAN

While you sit on an elephant you will be able
to break through your neighbour's hedge.
MALAYALAM (INDIA)

101

A stationary stone gathers moss.
RUSSIAN

Standing ponds gather dirt.
SCOTTISH

A tar dealer smells of tar.
RUSSIAN

The man with nostrils is 'Mr Nose'
amongst the noseless.
HINDI

TRADES AND PROFESSIONS

*Business-people don't get good press:
according to many of the following
they're all out to get you.*

Whoever has never seen a tiger, let him
look at a cat; and whoever has never seen
a robber, let him look at a butcher.
URDU

Look the other way when the girl
in the teahouse smiles.
JAPANESE

Carpenters and joiners are cursed by God.
RUSSIAN

He who sells poison uses a flowery signboard.
HUNGARIAN

If there were no bad taste,
goods would not be sold.
CHILEAN

Early to bed, early to rise, ain't never
no good if you don't advertise.
NORTH AMERICAN

The three learned professions live by roguery
on the three parts of man: the doctor
mauls our bodies, the parson starves our
souls, and the lawyer ensnares our minds.
ENGLISH

Badly cut hair is two men's shame.
DANISH

An honest miller has a thumb of gold.
ENGLISH

There is no greater thief than a master tailor.
RUSSIAN

The plough is king, the shop is queen; every
other business has the mark of hell.
PUNJABI

There is no monkey, but is mischievous;
no woman, but is a tattler; and
no silversmith, but is a thief.
SINHALESE

Thrash your apprentice while he has
not yet broken the water jug.
BULGARIAN

A truthful courtesan is as great
a miracle as a square egg.
JAPANESE

Barbers, doctors, pleaders, prostitutes
— all must have cash down.
INDIAN

Those who wear pearls do not know how
often the shark bites the legs of the diver.
ETHIOPIAN

LAW AND ORDER

Mankind seems united in its distrust of all things legal. Has no-one got a good word for lawyers?

Kick an attorney downstairs and
he will stick to you for life.
ENGLISH

The court is straight, but the judge is crooked.
RUSSIAN

The goat sued the wolf and all that was
left of him was his beard and horns.
UKRAINIAN

The houses of lawyers are roofed
with the skins of litigants.
WELSH

God wanted to chastise man
so he sent lawyers.
RUSSIAN

The law is like a cobweb: a beetle breaks
through, but a fly is caught.
CZECH

Many hares are hunted who
haven't eaten cabbages.
POLISH

He who goes to law should have
three bags: one of papers, one of
money, and one of patience.
FRENCH

110

The law has a nose of wax.
CZECH

When something falls into the hands of the
painter or the lawyer, white becomes black.
JAPANESE

Punishment ought to be like salad
— more oil than vinegar.
GERMAN

The Jew ruins himself with Passovers,
the Moor with wedding feasts, and
the Christian with lawsuits.
SPANISH

A piece of paper blown by the wind
into the law-court may in the end only
be drawn out again by two oxen.
CHINESE

A lawyer and a cartwheel
must be well greased.
GERMAN

The better lawyer, the worse Christian.
DUTCH

He that builds bridges and repairs roads will
become blind in both eyes; he that commits
murder and arson will enjoy long life.
CHINESE

112

Judges should have big ears and small hands.
GERMAN

KILL OR CURE!

Is there a doctor in the house? According to the following, you'd better hope there isn't!

First farming, next trade, last service,
or at least begging: if you cannot
obtain alms learn to be a doctor.
MARATHI

The inexperienced physician
makes a lumpy churchyard.
CZECH

Health goes in poods and
comes back in zolotniks.
RUSSIAN

A healthy poor man is half a rich one.
CHINESE

115

The gentle-handed doctor
makes a stinking wound.
FRENCH

The doctor's errors are covered with
earth; our own mistakes, with love.
GERMAN

A darned shirt and a stomach full
of drugs cannot last long.
ALBANIAN

If you wish to die soon make
your physician your heir.
ROMANIAN

If you have a father who is a physician,
send him to the house of your enemy.
PORTUGUESE

Death is the poor man's best physician.
IRISH

Bleed him and purge him; if he dies, bury him.
SPANISH

Only a doctor can kill you without punishment.
HUNGARIAN

Pay the doctor, praise the Lord.
JAMAICAN

God heals and the doctor gets the money.
FLEMISH

The doctor cures the sick
man who does not die.
JAPANESE

The smoker is brother to the dog.
RUSSIAN

There's a cure for everything
except stark dead.
SCOTTISH

Rhubarb and patience work wonders.
GERMAN

There is medicine in the house:
Alas! We must die.
HINDI (INDIAN)

A chemist's white bill is like
a dark autumn night.
RUSSIAN

119

The death of a thousand patients
makes a physician.
BENGALI

We must fear a doctor as well as a traitor.
TAMIL

Many doctors – death accomplished.
CZECH

LOVE AND MARRIAGE

Observations on the pleasures and perils of courtship and the – seemingly – mostly dire consequences of wedlock.

The dog that intends to bite, growls; the
bee that intends to sting, hums; but
a girl only makes her eyes sparkle.
POLISH

Who can forbid to a cat the top of
the oven, or a boy to a girl?
LIVONIAN

Love is a donkey freed of all tethers.
FULANI

Love and leprosy: few escape.
CHINESE

122

Coffee and love are best when they are hot.
GERMAN

Love enters man through his eyes;
woman through her ears.
POLISH

Frequent kisses end up in a baby.
HUNGARIAN

A timely marriage is like getting
up at the right time.
CZECH

One shouldn't think about it too much
when marrying or taking pills.
DUTCH

The hunt is a masculine ball, and
the ball is a feminine hunt.
GERMAN

Bachelor, a peacock; betrothed,
a lion; wedded, an ass.
SPANISH

Never marry for money; you'll
borrow it cheaper.
SCOTTISH

There were two brothers who had
brains, and a third who was married.
POLISH

To marry once is duty, twice is folly,
and the third time madness.
DUTCH

He who has had a wife deserves a
crown of patience, but he who has
had two deserves a straitjacket.
ITALIAN

In buying wives and melons
there is always danger.
SILESIAN

Matrimony and macaroni – if they
are not hot, they are not good.
GENOAN

The first night of marriage is
generally the last night of love.
SILESIAN

He who tells his wife all is but newly married.
SCOTTISH

If you hearken to your wife's first word, to
her second one you must listen forever.
BOSNIAN

Wives be like pilchards: when they be good they be middlin', and when they be bad they be bad.
ENGLISH

When your wife tells you to jump off a roof, pray to God that it is a low one.
SPANISH

A wife will be doubly attached if her chain is pleasant.
ANCIENT EGYPTIAN

One joins married people with their hands, and with their feet they run asunder.
GERMAN

127

A husband by the fireside is as
bad as a pain in the side.
SPANISH

There is peace in a house where the
husband is deaf and the wife is blind.
POLISH

No feast is without a roast piece; no real
torment is experienced until marriage.
IRISH

The wife carries her husband on her face;
the husband carries his wife on his linen.
BULGARIAN

If the husband gathers with a fan
and the woman scatters with a
spoon, there will never be a heap.
ALBANIAN

Better be quarrelling than lonesome.
IRISH

Consult thy wife and do the
reverse of what she advises.
TUNISIAN

The loved one is milk, the fiancée is butter
and the wife is seasoned cheese.
GERMAN

129

He who beats his oxen, beats his purse; but
he who beats his wife, beats his head.
BULGARIAN

My wife is my mule.
MONTENEGRIN

Hairy husband – smooth happiness.
ESTONIAN

A woman's clothes are the price
of her husband's peace.
BANTU (AFRICA)

A wife is like a giant.
GA (WEST AFRICA)

131

Trust your bitch sooner than your pretty wife.
BULGARIAN

Flowers will bloom on widows; maggots
will be hatched on widowers.
JAPANESE

Do not praise a day before sunset, a horse
before a year, and a wife before she's dead.
CZECH

A wife is twice kind – on her wedding
day and at her funeral.
RUSSIAN

A widow is as frisky as a horse
that has thrown a rider.
MALAYAN

THE GENERATION GAP

A few observations on the ageing process. As you might expect, it's mostly bad news, but not all.

134

The pearl weeps on the wrinkled neck.
GERMAN

Every gold tress is followed
by a fair moustache.
KURDISH

It is better to throw oneself into
a well than marry an old man.
TAMIL

He who lives longest has most old clothes.
ZULU (SOUTH AFRICA)

When one is past 30, one can about
half comprehend the weather.
CHINESE

Kill the elk in your youth if you would
lie in its skin in your old age.
FINNISH

Cursed is the young man of 100 and
blessed is the old man of 20.
ITALIAN

No man too old for an old maid.
JAMAICAN

136

Forty is the old age of youth;
50 is the youth of old age.
FRENCH

Beware of women with beards
and men without beards.
BASQUE

There's shelter beneath an old woman's beard.
SCOTTISH

When youth takes the scorpion for a
bedfellow, the aged go out on the roof.
CHINESE

Old bachelors and old maids are
either too good or too bad.
BASQUE

Ask the opinion of an older one and
a younger one than thyself, and
return to thine own opinion.
EGYPTIAN

The three best old things: an old lamb,
an old piglet and old seaweed.
IRISH

THE FAIRER SEX

Women feature in many proverbs – there are a few brickbats here, but some warm words too.

There are only two things a girl chooses
for herself – her potatoes and her lover.
DUTCH

If all girls are good, where do the
naughty old women come from?
FINNISH

The virtuous maid and the broken
leg must stay at home.
SPANISH

Three women and a goose make a market.
ITALIAN

A woman's advice is never worth having,
but no one but a fool refuses to follow it.
SPANISH

He that does not love a woman, sucked a sow.
ENGLISH

The longer the hair, the smaller the brain.
GERMAN

A pig is more impudent than a goat,
but a woman surpasses all.
IRISH

141

A fire, a woman, and a game
never say 'It is too much'.
SWISS

Women are saints in church, angels in the
street, devils in the kitchen, and apes in bed.
ENGLISH

A woman has the form of an angel, the heart
of a serpent and the sense of an ass.
GERMAN

She who wields a big wooden ladle rules all.
BHOJPURI (INDIAN)

Women are the whips of Satan.
IRAQI

The three small things that are best: a small
beehive, a small sheep and a small woman.
IRISH

With women, evil and cucumbers:
the smaller is the better.
HUNGARIAN

If a woman were as small as she is
good, one could make her a whole dress
and crown out of a parsley leaf.
FRENCH

A travelled woman is like a garden
trespassed by cattle.
MALAYAN

An old spinster is not worth more
than an unposted letter.
HUNGARIAN

God did not make woman from man's
head, that she should not rule over
him; nor from his feet, that she should
not be his slave; but from his side,
that she should be near his heart.
HEBREW

Never has a woman spoilt a thing with silence.
GERMAN

Silence is a beautiful jewel for a woman,
but she wears it so seldom.
DANISH

A woman's sword is her tongue,
and she does not let it rust.
CHINESE

All pretty maids are poisonous
pests; an enemy kills by hiding,
these by smiles and jests.
URDU

Even a fifty-tongued man cannot equal
a single-tongued woman at abusing.
SINHALESE

Woman is like an onion, nice and white to
look at, but when cut into — there is no
kernel, no heart, and one must cry.
GERMAN

Three kinds of men fail to understand women:
young men, old men and middle-aged men.
IRISH

147

A woman keeps secret only her age
and what she does not know.
BULGARIAN

Even Satan prays for protection from girls.
PUNJABI

The three dearest things: hens' eggs,
pork and an old woman's praise.
SCOTTISH

A maid that laughs is half taken.
ENGLISH

A fat woman is a quilt for the winter.
MULTANI (INDIAN)

Satisfy a dog with a bone and
a woman with a lie.
BASQUE

A woman spins even while she talks.
HEBREW

It is easier to guard a bush full
of hares than one woman.
ROMANIAN

Without women, men were but ill-licked cubs.
FRENCH

Obedience to a woman is the avenue of hell.
TUNISIAN

The three animals that spend the most time
over their toilet are cats, flies and women.
FRENCH

A hundred men can make an encampment,
but it takes a woman to make a home.
CHINESE

KEEPING UP APPEARANCES

A few words on beauty, the lack of it, and why it might not matter.

151

Beauty's only skin deep, but
ugly goes to the bone.
ENGLISH

A combed head hides ugly feet.
IRISH

The beetle is a beauty in the
eyes of its mother.
EGYPTIAN

The dowry goes with the wind and
the ugliness stays with the wife.
IRISH

If you are ugly, be winsome.
EGYPTIAN

No sow is so dirty that she can't
find a boar to kiss her.
GERMAN

A good-looking wife is the world's;
an ugly one, your own.
MARATHI (INDIAN)

In the eyes of the lover, pockmarks are dimples.
JAPANESE

To a co-wife, a fairy is uglier than a goblin.
URDU (INDIAN)

The thicker the veil, the less worth lifting.
TURKISH

It is the melancholy face that
gets stung by the bee.
JAPANESE

All the world's a camera — look
pleasant, please.
NORTH AMERICAN

OPEN HOUSE

Proverbs on homes and hospitality; with some sage advice for houseguests thrown in.

The fish and the guest go bad on the
third day and must be thrown out.
BASQUE

People of 70 you should not keep overnight,
and do not invite a person of 80 to sit down.
CHINESE

When you go to a friend's house,
leave your stomach behind.
GUYANESE

God bless him who pays short visits.
GERMAN

Let the guests at the table be three,
or four — at the most, five.
GREEK

158

A guest is a fowl — he will soon
have his neck wrung.
BONDEI (TANZANIA)

Always put the stranger near the danger.
IRISH

You may laugh at a friend's roof; don't
laugh at his sleeping accommodation.
BONDEI (EAST AFRICA)

A miserable bush is better than the open field.
MANX

You must show haste over three things only:
to bury your dead, to marry your daughter
and to set meat before strangers.
IRAQI

If your wife's relations arrive, open the
gate; if your own arrive, shut the gate.
RUSSIAN

The guest who outstays his fellow
guests loses his overcoat.
CHINESE

A new house should be lived in the
first year by an enemy, the second by
a friend and the third by yourself.
DUTCH

For one or two days, a guest; on the
third, the misfortune of one's life!
URDU

Better put a cockroach in the corner
of your house than a lodger.
ESTONIAN

Better to fill your house with stones
than to have a stranger in it.
KASHMIRI

He who invites storks must have frogs.
GERMAN

161

LITTLE DARLINGS

Advice on offspring, how to rear them, and what you can expect when they grow up.

Small children eat porridge; big
ones eat their parents' hearts.
CZECH

At ten years, a wonder child; at 15, a
talented youth; at 20, a common man.
JAPANESE

Many children, wide ears.
ESTONIAN

A busy mother makes an idle daughter.
PORTUGUESE

A poor family rearing a child is oppressed
by poverty for three years.
CHINESE

Spank small buttocks that large
buttocks may not be flogged.
BULGARIAN

An only daughter becomes a
bitch, an only son a dog.
ESTONIAN

The love of a child is like water in a basket.
ARGENTINEAN

When a daughter is born it is as though
seven thieves had got into the larder.
POLISH

The first cot is nothing, the second is
enough, and the third is senseless.
AFGHANISTANI

Children suck their mother when they're
young; their father when they're old.
JAMAICAN

If you love your son, give him plenty of cudgel;
if you hate him, cram him with dainties.
CHINESE

Happy is she who has borne a daughter;
a boy is the son of his mother-in-law.
TSWANA (SOUTH AFRICA)

Comb your daughter's hair until she is 12;
safeguard her until she is 16; after 16 say
'thank you' to whomsoever will wed her.
CZECH

Daughters and dead fish are
not keeping wares.
SCOTTISH

A house full of daughters is a
cellar full of sour beer.
DUTCH

A strong man lives by the price of his hire, but the weak lives by the price of his children.
ANCIENT BABYLONIAN

It is easier to bear a child once a year than to shave every day.
RUSSIAN

HAPPY FAMILIES

Most people have relatives, but whether you'd want them is another matter – apart from mothers, that is: everyone likes mum.

One may give up a father though he
be a magistrate, but not a mother
though she be a beggar.
CHINESE

A motherless child is like a
curry without onions.
TELEGU (INDIA)

An ounce of mother is worth a ton of priest.
SPANISH

The greatest love is mother love;
after that, comes a dog's love; after
that, the love of a sweetheart.
POLISH

When the mother dies, the
father becomes an uncle.
RUSSIAN

Better a penny than a brother.
WELSH

On earth there are four poisonous
things: the sun in the clouds, the wind
coming through an opening, a scorpion's
tail and a stepmother's heart.
CHINESE

Eat and drink with your relatives,
but do no business with them.
BOSNIAN

Fool your wife, use your bride, teach your children to eat coal.
ESTONIAN

The dog is my friend, my wife is my enemy, and my son is my master.
ARGENTINEAN

A mother-in-law, like the Yucca tree, is useful underground.
CUBAN

The death of a mother and a stone seat hurt with time.
ETHIOPIAN

I speak to you, O daughter-in-law, so
that you may hear, O neighbour.
EGYPTIAN

He that marries a widow with three
daughters marries four thieves.
ENGLISH

We were already 20 in the family, so
my grandmother had a baby.
SPANISH

Two brothers against a bear; two
brothers-in-law at a milk pudding.
RUSSIAN

Nobody's family can hang up the
sign 'Nothing the matter here'.
CHINESE

There is always a dirty spoon in every family.
GEORGIAN

He that has no fools, knaves, or beggars in
his family was begot by a flash of lightning.
ENGLISH

For the good stepmother there is a
golden chair in the Garden of Eden.
YIDDISH

Never rely on the glory of the morning,
nor the smiles of your mother-in-law.
JAPANESE

Parents are never in the wrong.
CHINESE

'Uncle' as long as he can be of use to us,
'Aunt' as long as there is buttermilk.
MARATHI (INDIAN)

In the time of need the pig is called uncle.
ALBANIAN

Confide in an aunt and the world will know.
CZECH

The man who has got a good son-in-law
has found a son, but he who has met
with a bad one has lost a daughter.
FRENCH

A son-in-law is as honey, a son as wormwood.
BULGARIAN

If you have no devil in the house,
take in a son-in-law.
RUSSIAN

He who eats alone, coughs alone.
EGYPTIAN

DISUNITED NATIONS

Stand by for some serious sniping and stereotyping. With rare exceptions, it seems that no-one has a good word for anyone.

177

When you shake hands with a
Greek, count your fingers.
ALBANIAN

If a man of Naresh has kissed
thee, count thy teeth.
HEBREW

When a snake gets warm on ice, then
a German will wish well to a Czech.
CZECH

Every man loves his own
country, even if it be hell.
IRAQI

If a Spaniard sings he is either
mad or penniless.
SPANISH

If you beat a Russian he can
even make you a watch.
RUSSIAN

The Englishman has intelligence at
the end of his fingers, the Frenchman
at the end of his tongue.
RUSSIAN

When the Ethiopian is white, the
French will love the English.
ENGLISH

Beware the horns of a bull, the heel of a
horse, and the smile of an Englishman.
IRISH

If a Bengali is a man, what is a devil?
PUNJABI

The moon is the Cossacks' sun.
RUSSIAN

When you have cut a Gypsy in ten
pieces you have not killed him – you
have only made ten Gypsies.
ROMANI

A Polish bridge, a Bohemian monk, a Swabian
nun, an Austrian soldier, Italian reverence
and German fasting are worth a bean.
GERMAN

Hang a German, even if he is a good man.
RUSSIAN

If you can deal with an Armenian,
you can deal with the Devil.
IRAQI

When God made the world he sent to the
Poles some reason and the feet of a gnat, but
even this little was taken away by a woman.
RUSSIAN

A demon took a monkey to wife – the result of
which, by the grace of God, was the English.
PUNJABI

A Scotsman is one who keeps the Sabbath,
and every other thing he can lay hands on.
NORTH AMERICAN

The friendship of the French is like their
wine, exquisite but of short duration.
GERMAN

A Turk, a parrot and a hare; these
three things are never satisfied.
INDIAN

Trust a Brahman before a snake, and a snake
before a harlot, and a harlot before an Afghan.
INDIAN

Do not trust a Hungarian unless he
has a third eye in his forehead.
CZECH

The Italians are wise before the
deed, the Germans in the deed and
the French after the deed.
ENGLISH

Beat a Chinaman enough and
he will speak Tibetan.
TIBETAN

The potatoes would be dug, washed, cooked
and eaten by the Ulsterman while the
Munsterman was saying 'potatoes'.
IRISH

An Irishman half-intoxicated, an Englishman with his belly full, and a Scotsman hungry are at their best.
IRISH

Adam and Eve spoke their love in Persian; and the angel who drove them out of Paradise spoke Turkish.
IRAQI

Hit him again, for he is Irish.
MANX

War with all the world, and peace with England.
SPANISH

185

The Greeks only tell the truth once a year.
RUSSIAN

What an Englishman cares to invent, a Frenchman to design, or a German to patch together, the stupid Pole will buy.
POLISH

The English have one hundred religions, but only one sauce.
FRENCH

Happy nations have no history.
BELGIAN

THE BEST OF ENEMIES

A few words on quarrels and the quarrelsome.

He on whose head we would break
a coconut never stands still.
YORUBA (WEST AFRICA)

May God rid me of my friends;
I can rid myself of my enemies.
CZECH

If the nose was not between the
eyes, they would eat each other.
GEORGIAN

There are two presents to be made to
an enemy: hot shot and cold steel.
CORSICAN

Two lords are going to have a fight
— farmers lend your hair!
CZECH

In a fight, sweetmeats are not distributed.
HINDI

Even in the other world we shall have to serve
the gentry, for they will be in the cauldrons
and we shall have to stoke the fires.
RUSSIAN

When the shepherds quarrel,
the cheese shows it.
BASQUE

In the house of an enemy have
his wife for a friend.
SPANISH

Kill many men with many weapons, for
a murderer's tool becomes known.
GURKHA

If you hate a man, let him live.
JAPANESE

The scabbard of my blue steel
is the liver of my enemy.
TIBETAN

HIDDEN DEPTHS?

On their first reading, many sayings aren't as clear as they might be, but a deeper meaning is sometimes revealed after a little meditation.

191

Mix thyself with bran and thou
shalt be eaten by pigs.
BOSNIAN

He who gives you a bone does
not wish to see you dead.
SPANISH

The rhinoceros which has no calf
takes itself to the muddy pool.
CHUANA (SOUTH AFRICA)

He who takes a step longer than his leg,
only accomplishes half his journey.
CORSICAN

192

The tongue is safe though in
the midst of 30 teeth.
SINHALESE

A dry bone is never licked.
ALBANIAN

A dealer in onions is a good judge of leeks.
FRENCH

If one pierces the nose, tears
come out of the eyes.
THAI

193

Don't sell the fox skin in the wood.
ROMANIAN

To be worth 100 ducats the donkey
must have good appearances.
BASQUE

On the bog, the fly is an admiral.
GERMAN

The love of the woodworm eats away crucifixes.
ITALIAN

Custom is rust that mocks at every file.
CZECH

Better keep under an old hedge than
creep under a new furze-bush.
ENGLISH

The frog saw how horses were shod,
so she also lifted up her foot.
SLOVENIAN

Don't talk small to a dwarf.
CHINESE

He who eats flax seeds eats his own shirt.
GREEK

He who dresses with a needle
undresses with a knife.
FINNISH

There is no art in beating foam.
GERMAN

Were it eatable it would not be hanging.
BULGARIAN

Cripples are always great doers
— break your leg and try.
SCOTTISH

The pig which is once seen in the crevice
of the fence is accused of all faults.
FINNISH

Kindness to the starfish is
as wind in the desert.
CHINESE

Sometimes one must let turnips be pears.
GERMAN

197

A muscle at home; a parrot abroad.
MAORI

He who enters a whirlwind
will depart as an ant.
BORNEO

When a child gets its teeth, the mother
should sell her skirt to buy it wine.
GERMAN

Better all black than just ink
splashed all around.
MALAYAN

Many complaints have made
the giant lizard deaf.
DUALA (WEST AFRICA)

When the butcher dies do you suppose
we shall eat our pork with bristles on?
CHINESE

If an ass goes astray, it may be
found near a ruinous wall.
TAMIL

A stranger is like rain, he strikes
you and passes on.
EAST AFRICAN

When a donkey is well off, he goes dancing on ice.
CZECH

A full sack cocks its ears.
ITALIAN

As soon as a cow has an udder of silver
she will quickly get golden nipples.
RUSSIAN

To the pig a carrot is a present.
GERMAN

What a pleasure to sit in the fire
having on strange trousers.
ESTONIAN

When the mouse eats the stone pot,
the pumpkin skin gets alarmed.
EWE (WEST AFRICA)

If you wish to follow people, drink wine; if
you wish to follow ducks, drink water.
GERMAN

A calf that goes with a pig will eat excrement.
TAMIL

His tongue is not burnt with porridge
who quarrels with old women.
FINNISH

202

He who sows peas on the highway
doesn't get all the pods into the barn.
DANISH

Better the gurgling of a camel
than the prayers of a fish.
EGYPTIAN

Give a dog an appetising name, and eat him.
CHINESE

He who refuses the sauce, refuses the bean.
EAST AFRICAN

O LUCKY MAN

*Forget talent, brains and good looks;
according to most of these proverbs
all you need is a four-leaf clover.*

Throw the fortunate man into the Nile and
he will come out with a fish in his mouth.
EGYPTIAN

He who is lucky gets piglets from his dog.
GERMAN

Sit not idle for your luck sits with you.
ROMANIAN

Luck is the idol of the idle.
ENGLISH

Good luck is an eel in the pond of fools.
RUSSIAN

A broken kettle never falls from its hook.
ITALIAN

The lucky man loses his wife,
the unlucky one his horse.
GEORGIAN

Many a time a good man fell on a cow pat.
IRISH

He who has got luck need only sit
at home with his mouth open.
GERMAN

If the swing goes forwards it
will come backwards too.
SINHALESE

Luck, like women, likes fools best.
NORWEGIAN

Give me, mother, luck at birth — then throw
me, if you will, on the rubbish heap.
BULGARIAN

The world is like a dancing girl: it
dances to everyone for a little time.
EGYPTIAN

MONEY, MONEY, MONEY

Words on wealth – with advice on how to keep what you've got, and grab what you've not.

Debts are like children: the smaller
they are, the more they scream.
SPANISH

A rich man's sickness and a poor man's
pancake are smelt a long way off.
FLEMISH

There is no economy in going to bed early
to save candles if the results be twins.
CHINESE

If a man is a miser he will certainly
have a prodigal son.
CHINESE

Praise the sorceress who adds to your larder.
POLISH

A miser is like a sow – useful only when dead.
CZECH

Lending to a spendthrift is like pelting a
trespassing dog with meat dumplings.
CHINESE

He who has gold is beloved, though
he be a dog, and a son of a dog.
TUNISIAN

211

The fear of want is worse than want itself.
POLISH

Copper money makes rusty love.
RUSSIAN

If your house is burning, its debts are
escaping through the chimney.
BULGARIAN

A pig on credit makes a good
winter and a bad spring.
PORTUGUESE

A beautiful woman smiling
means a purse weeping.
ITALIAN

Who is not strong at 20, married at 30
and rich at 40 is a complete fool.
UKRAINIAN

The flow of cash is better than
the sweetmeats of credit.
IRAQI

Three failures and a fire make
a Scotsman's fortune.
SCOTTISH

Skilful thefts appear like earnings;
unskilful earnings appear like thefts.
MALAYAN

Nothing seems expensive on credit.
CZECH

Does your neighbour's presence
annoy you? Lend him money!
ITALIAN

Rich gamblers and old trumpets are rare.
GERMAN

Accept even chaff and a sterile
goat from him who pays badly.
CZECH

215

A purse without money is called leather.
GENOAN

'Mr Immortal' is dead, 'Mr Possessor-of-Wealth' is begging, 'Mrs Riches' is gathering cow-dung cakes, so 'Mr Owner-of-Nothing' is best of all.
MARATHI

Brotherhood is brotherhood, but a kid is always worth half a crown.
IRAQI

A man may be a brother, but he should pay for his cheese.
SERBIAN

Although we are brothers, our
purses are not sisters.
BULGARIAN

Don't throw your prosperity out of the
door with a spade, while your husband is
bringing it in the window with a spoon.
ENGLISH

An heir's sobbing is laughing in disguise.
BULGARIAN

A fool and his goods are soon parted; a wise
man and his poverty always remain united.
RUSSIAN

Love, a cough, smoke and money
cannot long be hid.
FRENCH

'Mr Oh-Dear' put his savings aside,
and 'Mr Hurrah' spent them.
CZECH

With money you can even buy rabbit-cheese.
ROMANIAN

He who hoards today and tomorrow, and by
constant hoarding has bought a new umbrella,
finds that suddenly a strong wind arises and
leaves nothing but a bare bamboo stick.
CHINESE

COME ALL YE FAITHFUL

Priests, nuns and monks seem to have a poor reputation – almost as bad as lawyers!

219

In the primitive Church there were
chalices of wood and priests of gold; in
the modern Church there are chalices
of gold and priests of wood.
GERMAN

Malta would be a delightful place
if every priest was a tree.
MALTESE

There are three bloodsuckers in this world:
the bug, the flea and the Brahman.
INDIAN

If the wolf stayed in the forest and
the monk in the monastery, they
would not get such a bad name.
GERMAN

If you are looking for the priest, enquire
from the innkeeper, not the sexton.
BULGARIAN

Beware the foreparts of a woman, the hind
parts of a mule, and all sides of a priest.
ENGLISH

It is not necessary for priests to marry
as long as peasants have wives.
GERMAN

The clergyman's son is the Devil's grandson.
BULGARIAN

Do not blame God for having created the tiger,
but thank Him for not having given it wings.
ETHIOPIAN

It takes more than a hood and a
sad face to make a monk.
ALBANIAN

When the nuns dance, the Devil does not weep.
ROMANIAN

God gives us nuts, but He
does not crack them.
GERMAN

If the prayers of dogs were accepted,
bones would rain from the sky.
TURKISH

There are some gods that abandon men
— they are the gods that know men.
JAPANESE

If you wish to enquire where there is good wine,
enquire where the priests and monks go.
BULGARIAN

Seek the brave in prison and the
stupid amongst the clergy.
RUSSIAN

An honest magistrate has lean clerks;
a powerful god has fat priests.
CHINESE

Give a Brahman clarified butter
and he will wriggle with delight.
BHOJPURI (INDIA)

There are three things I have never
seen: the eye of an ant, the foot of a
snake, and the charity of a mullah.
IRAQI

God does not shave — why should I?
BULGARIAN

God made the Earth, but the
Dutch made Holland.
DUTCH

God is not sinless, he created the world.
BULGARIAN

PROVERBS FOR PESSIMISTS

Assorted doom and gloom. Don't read these if you want to be cheered up.

If misfortune has not found you,
wait a minute – you will find it.
BULGARIAN

Peculiar people's children are usually failures.
CZECH

The best swimmers are drowned.
BULGARIAN

If you wish to be blamed, marry; if
you wish to be praised, die.
OROMO (NORTH AFRICA)

If we go forward we die; if we go backward
we die; better go forward and die.
ZULU

Buy beef, you buy bone; buy
land, you buy rock-stone.
JAMAICAN

Friendship lasts as long as
the kitchen smokes.
GERMAN

The poor man's cow and the rich man's
son are the two things that will die.
IRISH

Distrust your friend, he'll stuff
your hide with straw.
TURKIC

A blind cat catches only dead rats.
CHINESE

He who depends on the people
hangs from a tree.
GERMAN

The fox's last hole is the furrier's shop.
ARMENIAN

He who thinks he is raising a mound
may in reality only be digging a pit.
CHINESE

He who builds on the favours of the great,
advances towards fortune mounted on a crab.
GERMAN

He who washes a beautiful
goat seldom milks it.
TSWANA (SOUTH AFRICA)

When rubles fall from heaven, there is no sack;
when there is a sack, the rubles do not fall.
RUSSIAN

From the drop of water through the roof, and death through the door, there is no escape.
ALBANIAN

Almonds come to those who have no teeth.
CHINESE

Life is an onion which one peels crying.
FRENCH

A man can hang himself from his own tree as well as from his neighbour's.
RUSSIAN

The biggest drops of rain fall on the bald head.
GERMAN

Man is a leather bottle full of wind.
LATIN

Death carries a fat tsar on his
shoulders as easily as a lean beggar.
RUSSIAN

He needs a long candle that
awaits the death of another.
FINNISH

The art of dying can never
be studied too much.
SWEDISH

233

Adam and Eve ate the apple, and I, who
didn't taste it, have to pay for it.
GERMAN

We come and cry, and that is life; we
cry and go, and that is death.
FRENCH

We are born crying, live complaining,
and die disappointed.
ENGLISH

At birth we cry, at death we see why.
BULGARIAN

At the camping place where there's water,
there's no grazing; where there's grazing,
there's no water; where there are no
mosquitoes, the wind is bitter; when you've
got your father, your mother isn't there.
CHINESE

He who is not yet dead is not
yet clear of defects.
KENYAN

Dreams give wings to fools.
HEBREW

Every hour that passes wounds
us, and the last kills us.
SPANISH

Be very humble: the hopes of men are worms.
HEBREW

The most important thing in
life is to get buried well.
CHINESE

The squirrel climbs up the painted
fir and dies of hunger.
RUSSIAN

He who seeks a constant friend
goes to the cemetery.
RUSSIAN

There are two good people: one of them
is dead, the other one was not born.
ESTONIAN

It is better to die two years too soon
than to live one year too long.
CHINESE

When you've made your bed
everyone wants to lie in it.
RUSSIAN

237

Drink and sing: an inch before us is black night.
JAPANESE

WISE WORDS

A selection of proverbs containing nuggets of good, common sense advice… at least, I think they do.

Better a wee fire to warm you,
than a big fire to burn you.
SCOTTISH

To a man who wears sandals the whole
world seems covered in leather.
TELEGU (INDIA)

The man who tickles himself can
laugh when he chooses.
GERMAN

You don't know what there is in a man
till you have hit him on the nose.
NORWEGIAN

Govern a great nation as you
would cook a small fish.
CHINESE

He who waits for another's soup eats it cold.
SICILIAN

When puss gone, rat take house.
JAMAICAN

He who has nobody to tie him
up should not go mad.
YORUBA

Whoever pats scorpions with the hand
of compassion receives punishment.
IRAQI

Do not burn down your house to
inconvenience even your wife's mother.
CHINESE

Crab walk too much, he get in crab soup.
CREOLE

A child that can walk is a god
to the child in the cradle.
INDIAN

A dog does not long remain tied to a sausage.
GERMAN

Nobody measures the river
with both of his feet.
GA (WEST AFRICA)

One 'take this' is better than
ten 'God help you'.
GERMAN

The biggest help is help, and even
the smallest help is help.
IRISH

Two men are frightened of an unloaded gun.
BULGARIAN

A dog will remember a three days' kindness
for three years; while a cat will forget
three years' kindness in three days.
JAPANESE

It is the tortoise that discounts
the value of a pair of fast legs.
JAPANESE

Creaking wagons are long in passing.
FRIESIAN (NETHERLANDS)

Mediocrity is climbing a molehill
without sweating.
ICELANDIC

In a bet there is a fool and a thief.
WALLOON (BELGIUM)

The little dog should cross the river first
before it curses the crocodile's mouth.
EWE (WEST AFRICA)

Never be boastful, someone may come
along who knew you as a child.
CHINESE

If you are not skilful in dancing,
then you can strike the gong.
BURMESE

When a bear is at your heels, do
not look for his footprints.
GREEK

If you would not be cheated, ask
the price at three shops.
CHINESE

Seize opportunity by the beard,
for it is bald behind.
BULGARIAN

See the candle light before you
blow out the match.
JAMAICAN

Measure nine times, cut once.
BULGARIAN

TAKE THEM OR LEAVE THEM

Some traditional sayings appear of doubtful quality: kernels of curious observation or dubious advice. Take the following with a pinch of salt.

A friend spits into a friend's pocket.
ESTONIAN

Asthmatic people live long.
IRISH

Death is deaf.
SPANISH

If you are feeling nice – keep quiet.
POLISH

To a fool the ice seems slippery.

LATVIAN

Beware of the man who swallows his phlegm.

SERBIAN

Beware of him who squints, or has red hair.

SERBIAN

Beware of a man with a long chin.

SPANISH

One should not board a ship without an onion.
DUTCH

Everything comes, even pie.
SERBIAN

A lame man copulates best.
GREEK

Do not throw stones into thin mud.
BULGARIAN

252

The little pig gets the big parsnip.
GUERNSEY

The empty house is full of noise.
BASQUE

He must have clean fingers who
would blow another's nose.
DANISH

SAY AGAIN?

Some of the following proverbs seem to have lost a little in translation, while others may refer to obscure local customs, practices and beliefs. Most seem completely incomprehensible. Any ideas?

255

A mother-in-law near the door is
like a cloak near a hedge.
ALBANIAN

He who cheats at cards should not
complain of peaches on his face.
POLISH

The size of your fish has made you disloyal.
MAORI

He who would make the hole under his
nose bigger must wear patched shoes.
DANISH

He who takes a raven for a companion
must not come off the dunghill.
ARMENIAN

He who fears cranes should not sow beans.
MALTESE

Does the ant ask favours of the hornbill?
DAYAK (INDONESIA)

You cannot buy honourable
rice from a dead uncle.
CHINESE

Baghdad is far away, but the foot-rule is here.
BOSNIAN

Don't trust the son of the cow.
IRISH

No one carrying elephant's flesh on his head
should look for crickets underground.
YORUBA (WEST AFRICA)

He who falls into the sea without
getting wet has to pay the penalty.
ITALIAN

An early bird wipes its beak; a
late one wipes its buttocks.
ESTONIAN

A man with soft ears is sure
to get them pulled.
MALAYAN

He who goes to the sea without
biscuits returns without teeth.
CORSICAN

Where you find a cow, you find a woman; and
where you find a woman, you find a brother.
IRISH

There belongs more to a bed than bare legs.
SCOTTISH

Where there is union, a bullet can swim.
BULGARIAN

In harvest time the rat has four wives.
HINDI

Eternity gives place to the salted cucumber.
RUSSIAN

He who feeds himself with a quill
must stick it behind his ear.
SILESIAN

He who would sleep well should fasten
his thoughts to the doorbell.
POLISH

A man's thigh becomes
diseased through itself.
HEBREW

Who has eaten the honey? He who
has a fly on his umbrella.
GREEK

261

A person waiting for hair is not bold.
WELSH

Boil a stone in butter and
its juice will be drunk.
IRISH

The housewife keeps the parrot,
the lover keeps the songbird, and
the thief keeps pigeons.
INDIAN

The rat could not enter his hole and
he tied a broom to his tail.
IRAQI

A grasshopper does not always
come when one breaks a string.
GREEK

He puts his cheese in a bottle and
rubs the cheese on the outside.
IRAQI

One who is cowless must be his own dog.
IRISH

Don't let your sorrows come
higher than your knees.
SWEDISH

When your head aches, anoint your knee-pans.
SPANISH

When you take a squirrel out of the
water, it contrives a plot against you.
DUALA (WEST AFRICA)

He who eats old bread will swim easily.
RUSSIAN

The law of heredity ran through the cat's eyes.
IRISH

An old man's skull is a raisin.
GREEK

During the cat's harvest, hens are deaf.
DUTCH

The pig that does not whine while
being carried, does not generate.
ESTONIAN

She is a foolish woman who
blames her own cabbage.
DANISH

Two hazelnuts make an army for the walnut.
SERBIAN

The morsel not toiled for
makes the neck white.
DUTCH

Shears make a child blind
and a knife one-eyed.
DANISH

What goes wrong in the stable
falls on the monkey's head.
INDIAN

If thou art satisfied with false munchings,
they are a diversion in thy saliva.
HEBREW

267

The stomach has no windows.
ALBANIAN

The doctor has ringworm on his nose.
INDIAN

Because of a beetle's hum the
sunset does not come.
ESTONIAN

A new government and a drum on a hen's back.
URDU

Unshakeable happiness does
not want a string.
ESTONIAN

Don't open your mouth until
a goose has flown in.
ICELANDIC

Feigned laughter ruins the teeth.
TAMIL

A farthing hag got her head
shaved for a penny.
INDIAN

The Gypsy church was made of
pork and the dogs ate it.
ROMANI

He who makes cream with his mouth,
must make butter with his nose.
GERMAN

Who can prevent the master getting
fleas with his gloves on?
LATVIAN

A good buttock finds a bench for itself.
ESTONIAN

270

The laugh of the rose makes the
nightingale lose its head.
GEORGIAN

The mountain made a great effort
and bought forth a mouse.
BULGARIAN

Milk the mosquito to serve your king.
BULGARIAN